CREATION

CREATION

Alister McGrath

Fortress Press
Minneapolis

CREATION

First Fortress Press Edition 2005

Scripture quotations are from the New Revised Standard Version Bible,
copyright © 1989 by the Division of Christian Education of the National Council
of the Churches of Christ in the USA and used by permission.

Cover art: *The Sower*, 1888 (oil on canvas) by Vincent van Gogh (c. 1853–90),
E. G. Bührle Collection, Zurich, Switzerland
Interior design and typesetting: Theresa Maynard
Cover design by Monica Capoferri

ISBN: 0-8006-3700-3

Manufactured in Belgium

09   08   07   06   05   1   2   3   4   5   6   7   8   9   10

contents

introduction

'You shall love the Lord your God with all your heart, with all your soul, and with all your mind' (Matthew 22.34–37). This is the greatest commandment of them all, the supreme responsibility for believers. With these striking words, Jesus set an agenda for Christian discipleship that has reverberated down the centuries. Every faculty that we possess should be caught up in the joy of growing in our faith, and becoming more faithful and effective Christian believers. We are to use every resource that God has given us to help us 'know Christ more clearly, love him more dearly, and follow him more nearly' (Richard of Chichester).

This process of growth and maturation is marked by a *discipleship of the mind*, in which we take the great themes of the Christian faith seriously, and explore their implications. Part of our task as Christians is to discover the riches of our faith for ourselves. In doing this, we discover the truth of one of the most remarkable pieces of Christian wisdom: it is in encountering and experiencing God that we finally discover ourselves. To know ourselves properly, we must first know God. Theological reflection thus leads to our personal enrichment and fulfilment, alongside a deepened appreciation of our faith.

There is a genuine intellectual excitement to wrestling with God. The great Christian theologian Augustine of Hippo (354–430) spoke of an '*eros* of the mind'. By this he meant a deep sense of longing to understand more about God's nature and ways, and the transformative impact of this process on people's lives. This short book aims to explain some of the central Christian ideas about the idea of 'creation' in simple and helpful terms, weaving these biblical themes together into a rich tapestry of faith and life.

Yet this book is about more than ideas, which often seem cold and impersonal, with little apparent relevance to knowing and loving God. How can learning the words of a catechism help anyone to rise in the presence of the living God, or lead a more effective life of service and care? How can reading a theology textbook lead us to worship? We must do more than simply think about our faith. It needs to percolate throughout our minds, hearts and souls, saturating every aspect of our existence. There is another discipleship that we must discover – *a discipleship of the imagination*, in which we allow the great themes of the Christian faith to control, nourish and delight our glorious vision of the God-created world.

This book uses carefully chosen illustrations to stimulate and inform both the believing mind and imagination. They are there to guide the 'sight of our imagination' (Ignatius Loyola) as we explore both the *truth* and *reality* of Christianity. Words and images – such as the meditations of John Donne and George Herbert, the theological reflections of the great writers of the Christian tradition, the frescoes of Michelangelo and the stunning landscapes of Bruegel and Rubens – will accompany us as we travel on this voyage of discovery, helping us to visualize the context in which the truths of the gospel are set.

We are often like people standing on the shore of a coral island, staring into the distance. We see the ocean stretching ahead of us, with its gently undulating waves caressing the shoreline. The surface of the water seems to be little more than a series of ripples, flashing in the sunlight. Yet beneath lies a living world of coral outcrops, richly populated with marine plants and fishes, darting colourfully in the sun-dappled sea. This book sets out to go beneath the surface of our faith, and gain a deeper appreciation of the beauty of its depths, through words and images.

Alister McGrath

encountering creation

1 encountering creation

'I believe in Christianity as I believe that the Sun has risen – not only because I see it, but because by it, I see everything else' (C. S. Lewis). These words help us understand why faith in God is so important to seeing and understanding the world, and our place within it. Yet faith is about more than just understanding. As Lewis points out, a 'believed idea' feels different from an idea that is not believed. Once the Christian worldview has been accepted as true, it leads to a 'special sort of imaginative enjoyment'. Beliefs, when grasped and trusted as real and true, possess an *aesthetic* quality, which allows us to appreciate, cherish and admire divine reality through our imaginations.

We see everything in the light of our vision of God. Believing in God is like putting on spectacles, which allow us to see the world in a special way. The doctrine of creation is like a lens bringing a vast landscape into sharp focus, or a map helping us grasp the features of the terrain around us. What exactly is this world in which we live? And what is our place within it? These are questions that arise naturally and properly as we think about the meaning of life, and what we must do if we are to be faithful disciples in the world. The Christian answer to such questions is lavish and deeply satisfying, weaving together a series of ideas to yield a richly coloured and patterned tapestry. One of these ideas is the doctrine of creation, the subject of this volume.

'*In the beginning, God created* . . .' These opening words of the Bible have had a powerful impact on shaping the mind of the Church. We find them in Christian creeds, confessions and catechisms. They have stimulated intense reflection on its implications. The really important point made by the doctrine of creation is that everything owes its origins to God. Neither the world, nor we ourselves, are accidental or pointless. Nor do we simply inhabit God's creation as if we could be indifferent to its beauty. Countless

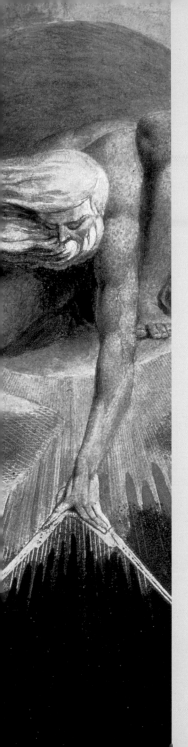

Christian writers of almost every theological hue stress that God created us to *enjoy* the creation.

The belief that God created the world triggers off lines of thought that lead to an enrichment of our understanding and imagination. Among those we shall be considering in this volume are:

> If God created the world, then something of his wisdom and beauty is reflected in that created order. We see the glory of the creator in the beauty of the creation.

> The created order is God's, not ours. We must learn to respect it as something within which we live, and whose care has been entrusted to us.

Yet this is to jump ahead of our discussion. The first major issue we need to explore is what we mean when we talk about God's 'creating' the world. This theme resonates throughout the Bible. Perhaps one of the most significant points the Old Testament makes is that *nature is not divine*. Thus the Genesis creation account stresses that God created the moon, sun and stars (Genesis 1.14–18). It is easy to miss the significance of this point. Many in the ancient world saw these heavenly bodies as divine, and worshipped or feared them as a result. Some believed that they exercised a deep, possibly sinister, influence over human destiny. The Old Testament insists that, since they were *created* by God, they are *subordinate* to God. We need not be afraid of them. They are subject to God as their creator. The doctrine of creation thus offers liberation for those who believe that their fate is subject to mysterious astral forces over which they have no control. It assures us that we need not fear any aspect of creation, if we know and are known by its creator.

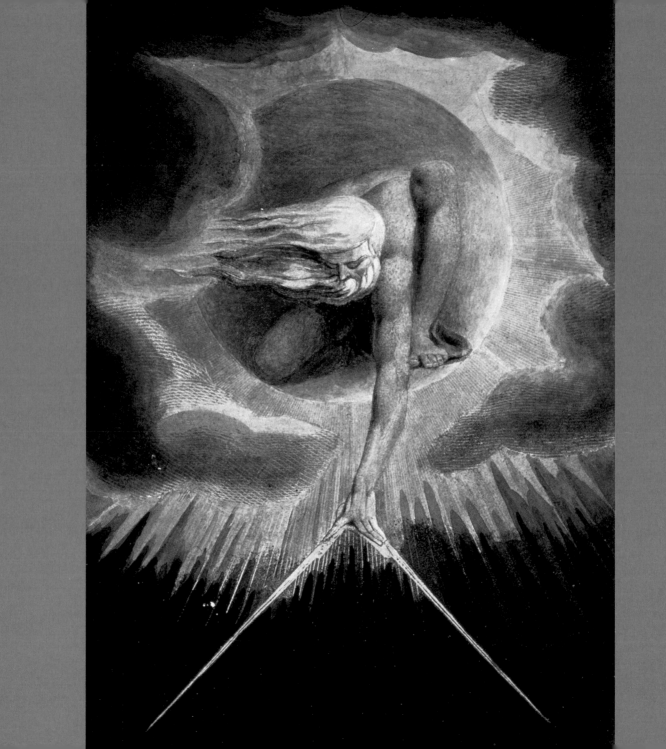

The biblical writers emphasize the care of God for every aspect of the created order, above all humanity. Having lovingly fashioned the world, God does not abandon it, but continues to care for it. The God who created the world may be known, trusted and relied upon. This point is made by Isaiah in a passage which reassures the people of Jerusalem, then held captive in Babylon, that they have not been forgotten by their God (Isaiah 40.27–28).

> Why do you say, O Jacob, and speak, O Israel,
> 'My way is hidden from the LORD, and my right is disregarded by
> my God'?
> Have you not known? Have you not heard?
> The LORD is the everlasting God, the Creator of the ends of the earth.
> He does not faint or grow weary.

Jesus continued this line of thought in the Sermon on the Mount. If God cares for the birds of the air and the lilies of the field – as he surely does! – how much more will he care for the needs of his people? They must never be anxious (Matthew 6.25–34).

To believe in God as our creator thus affects the way we live in the world. It is not simply a notional adjustment to the way we view things, which makes little difference to everyday life. Rather, it gives us a 'big picture' of our place in this world, and above all in relation to God. Martin Luther (1483–1546) knew of the importance of the practical application of Christian beliefs, and developed the 'Catechism' as a means of educating ordinary people about the implications of their belief. Here is Luther explaining in simple terms what it means to believe in God as creator:

I believe that God created me, along with all creatures. He gave me my body and soul, eyes, ears and all the other parts of my body, my mind and all my senses, and preserves them as well. He gives me clothing and shoes, food and drink, house and land, spouse and children, fields, animals and all I own. Every day He abundantly provides everything I need to nourish this body and life. He protects me against all danger, shields and defends me from all evil. He does all this because of His pure, fatherly and divine goodness and His mercy, not because I have earned it or deserved it.

The doctrine also calls us to mission. The biblical writers knew that to believe that God was the creator of the entire earth – not just Israel! – has evangelistic implications. If this was the God of all the earth – and not just of one tiny geographical region – then the day would come when 'the earth will be filled with the knowledge of the glory of the LORD, as the waters cover the sea' (Habakkuk 2.14).

But how are we to make sense of the idea of creation? How can we visualize the notion? It often seems very abstract. Down the ages, Christian theologians have developed images or models of creation, based on biblical originals. In what follows, we shall explore two of them – God as the architect of the world and God as an artist – and ask how they help us to understand this belief.

The image of God as an architect, already implicit in the Bible (Psalm 127.1), was given a new injection of energy during the long history of Christian reflection on the biblical material. The image helps us to visualize the fundamental Christian idea that the world is an ordered structure. The wisdom of the creator can thus be seen in the ordering of the world, in much the same way as the ingenuity of an architect can be seen in the design of a great building. Creation is thus about ordering, imposing structure upon reality.

Nature is emblazoned with the glory of God. It bears an eloquent, if silent, witness to God's wisdom, just as a great building bears witness to the genius of its designer. St Paul's Cathedral, London, is one of the greatest works of the architect Sir Christopher Wren (1631–1723). The original cathedral was destroyed during the Great Fire of London (1666), and had to be rebuilt. The task of designing the new building was entrusted to Wren. The spectacular new edifice was finally completed in 1710, and remains one of the most famous landmarks of London. There is no memorial to Wren in that cathedral. In its place, there is an inscription over its north door: 'If you are looking for a memorial, look around you.' The genius and wisdom of the architect can be seen in what he built.

In the same way, the wisdom of God can be discerned within the creation, which is a witness to the power and wisdom of its creator. 'The heavens are telling the glory of God' (Psalm 19.1). For this reason Celtic Christianity, celebrated for its love of nature, referred to the created world as the 'great cathedral', to be compared to the rather less impressive 'little cathedrals' constructed by human hands.

It is not surprising that such a visually rich theme should attract the attention of artists. One of William Blake's most striking and best-known

illustrations is the relief etching with watercolour known as *The Ancient of Days* (1794). This dramatic illustration represents Blake's attempt to capture something of the drama of the creation of all things. It appears as a frontispiece to his 1794 work *Europe: A Prophecy,* and was not known by any title until the art critic J. T. Snow gave it this name in 1828. Blake depicts God as one who creates the world in an orderly manner – note the measuring instrument God holds in his left hand. Blake here picks up on one of the great themes of the Christian tradition – that creation is about imposing order. God takes something that is formless, and shapes it into something structured.

Blake's imagery has its origins in the book of Job. This long and complex Old Testament work centres on the character of Job – someone who is reduced to misery, protest and anguish over the seeming meaninglessness of the world. Distressed by his wretchedness, three of his friends try to comfort him with various erudite (and occasionally rather opaque) arguments. Yet they fail to satisfy him.

The narrative then takes a dramatic turn. God 'answered Job out of the whirlwind' (Job 38.1) – an image which is clearly depicted in Blake's work of art. In the long speech that follows, God offers Job a panoramic view of the entire created order in all its immensity and grandeur – its seas, mountains and living creatures. The message of this great speech is clear: I, the God who made all these things, am here and care for you. Though you may not be able to grasp all that I have done, you may trust me in all things.

Yet Blake's *The Ancient of Days* conveys another message, too easily overlooked. One of Blake's great concerns was that the life of the human imagination might be impoverished and stunted through an excessive reliance on reason. Blake's illustration is partly a critique of the excessively rational approach to God as creator, which he especially associated with seventeenth-century writers such as Sir Isaac Newton through his mechanical model of the solar system. Newton's view of God and creation, Blake argued, was 'sheath'd in dismal steel'. Reality was now restricted to what could be measured. Both nature itself and God's work of creation were seen in purely mechanical terms. But what of spirituality and beauty? Something more was needed – something that would engage the human imagination, not exclude it.

The Old Testament prophets saw the way in which a potter created a vessel out of a formless mass of clay as a powerful analogy of God's creative action and power (Isaiah 29.16). God is thus like an artist, who creates a work of art from raw materials. Many Christian theologians have argued that God is like a sculptor or a painter – someone who crafts, shapes and weaves. Dorothy L. Sayers (1893–1957), now remembered mainly for her detective novels based on amateur aristocratic sleuth Lord Peter Wimsey, suggested that God could be thought of as the author of a book. Such an author, she argued, brought both characters and scenarios into existence, and communicated them in such a way that could influence the lives of others. This idea was well known to earlier Christian writers, who argued that God had authored two books – the 'book of Scripture' and the 'book of nature'– each of which revealed God in different, yet complementary, ways.

For this reason, Blake himself preferred to think of God as an artist – one who sought to engage the imagination, rather than merely the understanding. What God sought to communicate was as much *beauty* as *truth*. It was best and it was right, Blake argued, to see the natural world as God's work of art, evoking the believer's wonder and delight rather than mere assent to God's existence and wisdom.

Lord, help us to see your glory in the world around us, and to know you as our creator and redeemer.

We shall explore the relation between creation and the human sense of wonder soon. But first, we must consider the impact of the doctrine of creation on our attitude to the world around us.

 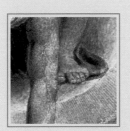 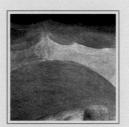 

tending the creation

One of the great quests of the Middle Ages was to find a magic formula or tool that would allow base metal to be turned into precious gold. The 'philosopher's stone' had the ability to transmute lesser things into something precious, and was ardently sought throughout this restless age. Other sources spoke of an 'elixir' – a liquid derived from this mysterious stone – which possessed the power to bring about physical and spiritual regeneration.

In his poem 'The elixir', the English poet George Herbert (1593–1633) used the image of the 'philosopher's stone' to help his readers appreciate the new vision of reality that knowing God brings to human life.

> This is the famous stone
> That turneth all to gold:
> For that which God doth touch and own
> Cannot for less be told.

By using such powerful imagery throughout his poem, Herbert points to the power of the Christian vision of God to transform the way we see things. The world is transmuted from a base metal to nothing less than gold. The natural order is no longer seen as something pointless and meaningless, having no purpose other than to satisfy our whims and needs. We now see it in a brilliant new light – as something that God 'doth touch and own', which cannot be 'told' (an older English way of expressing the idea of being 'reckoned' or 'valued') for anything less. When we see nature as God's creation, it changes not merely in *meaning* but in *value*. Earlier, we noted how God's work of creation could be compared to a work of art. News reports of international art auctions remind us that discovering the signature of a famous artist on a beautiful painting can completely transform its value.

This does not merely affect the way we think about the world. It ought also to change the way we behave towards it. It forces us to abandon any idea of the earth as our servant which we can exploit as we please. Instead, we are forced to think of the world as something wonderful and beautiful, created and loved by God, which we are called to tend, as Adam tended the garden of Eden.

The Christian doctrine of creation has four major implications for ecology:

The natural order, including humanity, is the result of God's act of creation, and is affirmed to be God's possession.

Humanity is distinguished from the remainder of creation by being created in the 'image of God'. This distinction is about the delegation of responsibility rather than the conferral of privilege. It does not encourage or legitimize environmental exploitation or degradation.

Humanity is charged with the tending of creation (as Adam was entrusted with the care of Eden – Genesis 2.15), in the knowledge that this creation is the cherished possession of God.

There is no basis for asserting that humanity has the 'right' to do what it pleases with the natural order. The creation is God's, and has been entrusted to us. We are to act as its guardian, not its exploiter.

Some environmentalist writers have suggested that Christianity is somehow responsible for the environmental crisis that has built up over recent decades. Back in the 1960s, the American writer Lyn White argued that

Christianity has given religious sanction to the human longing to dominate nature, and hence to exploit it. However, this claim is no longer taken unambiguously. Study after study has shown that the dominant approach of the Christian tradition is to respect the earth as something that God has entrusted to humanity.

If anything, it is the modern elimination of any religious dimension to nature that has led to its violation. The movement that we often call 'the Enlightenment' argued that it was utterly irrational and outdated to see the world in anything other than purely natural terms. The biblical idea of allowing land to rest for a year was dismissed as primitive superstition. Humanity was free to master and exploit nature. On this reading of things, the only justification that can be offered for environmental concern is that it will help the survival of humans or preserve landscapes which humans enjoy. But there is nothing *intrinsic* to nature itself that demands that it should be treated in this way.

Christianity takes a very different view. Nature cannot be 'told' – to use George Herbert's term – for anything less than the cherished creation and possession of the living and loving God. To love God entails loving what God loves. The Christian understanding of nature brings about its transvaluation, which must affect the way we treat it. Nature is to be esteemed as God's entrustment to us.

Yet it may also be valued for another reason – the Christian expectation of the final restoration of creation. Part of the Christian hope is that there will be a final act of consummation, in which the existing order will be renewed and refashioned to create a 'new heaven and a new earth' (Revelation 21.1). There will be a restoration of the harmony of Eden. This idea has exercised a deep appeal to the Christian imagination. Theologically, it stresses the continuity between creation and consummation, the first and the last things. Ecologically, it affirms that the conservation of the creation will play an important role in the future renewal of the earth, when God's kingdom finally comes.

Christian thinking about the future has been deeply shaped by two controlling images: a city (the new Jerusalem) and a garden (the new Eden). Like the great earthly city of Jerusalem itself, the restored creation will be a place of security and safety, in which God will dwell. This vision of the 'golden city' made a deep impression on the spirituality of the Middle Ages, as some of its great hymns make clear. Who can sing a hymn such as 'Jerusalem the Golden' without catching a glimpse of the vision of the New Jerusalem, which inspires us to continue on the journey of faith through life?

The word 'paradise' is often used to refer to the vision of the restored and renewed creation that awaits us in heaven. It seems to have its origins in the languages of the ancient Near East, particularly the Old Persian word *paradeida*, which means something like an enclosed garden or perhaps a royal park. The Greek word *paradeisos* – clearly borrowed from this Persian original – is often used in the writings of historians like Xenophon to refer to the great walled gardens of the royal palaces of Persian kings such as Cyrus. The original 'garden of Eden' (Genesis 2) is referred to as 'paradise' in Greek translations of the Old Testament. Heaven can be thought of as a restored garden of Eden.

The garden of Eden was seen as a place of fertility and harmony, where humanity dwelt in peace with nature and 'walked with God'. That idyllic state had been lost at the dawn of human history. Part of Israel's hopes and expectations for the future centred around the nostalgic longing for a restoration of this paradisiacal relationship with the environment and God. The prophet Hosea, writing in the eighth century before Christ, looks forward to a future transformation of the human situation. Human enmity against other humans has ended, and the integrity of the original created order has been restored.

> I will make for you a covenant on that day with the wild animals, the birds of the air, and the creeping things of the ground; and I will abolish the bow, the sword, and war from the land. (Hosea 2.18)

The prophet Joel depicts the future Israel as being like a new Eden. Its mountains will flow with wine, its hills will flow with milk and the dry river beds will be filled with pure clear water – just as Eden was surrounded and watered by its four great rivers:

> On that day the mountains shall drip sweet wine, the hills shall flow with milk, and all the stream beds of Judah shall flow with water; a fountain shall come forth from the house of the LORD and water the Wadi Shittim. (Joel 3.18)

A similar approach is found in the prophet Micah, who offers a vision of a future state in which the vineyard and fig tree serve as symbols of tranquillity and fertility (Micah 4.4).

One of the most interesting reworkings of the paradise theme is found in the prophecy of Ezekiel, dating from the time of the exile of the

people of Jerusalem in Babylon. Again, Ezekiel sees the anticipated restoration of Jerusalem in Edenic terms. For Ezekiel, the people of Jerusalem had brought their destruction and exile upon themselves by profaning the temple of the Lord, and failing to live up to their obligations as God's people. Yet Jerusalem will be restored, in a form that transcends the city and temple of earlier times. The land will be renewed and made fertile by a sacred healing river that flows eastwards, emptying into the Dead Sea. Ezekiel's vision of the New Jerusalem that will arise to replace the fallen, ruined city draws heavily upon paradisiacal imagery. A new paradise will be created within the walls of the restored city of God.

The huge success of John Milton's epic poem *Paradise Lost* (1667) led to intense artistic interest in depicting Eden as an idealized place of innocence – an unblemished creation, in which humans, animals and plants coexisted in harmony, and in close fellowship with God. Faced with the rather harsher reality around them, many preferred to seek solace in the past. Many artists rose to the challenge – perhaps none more so than Jan Bruegel (*c.* 1568–1625), who is known to have painted at least 106 versions of the Eden theme. Many of these were collaborations with Peter Paul

Rubens (1577–1640), widely regarded as the outstanding landscape artist of the period.

The illustration that accompanies this chapter was painted by Bruegel and Rubens at some time during the period 1610–15 in oil on a wood panel. The right-hand side of the painting is dominated by plants and animals, domestic and wild, including many exotic species. These are generally represented in pairs, perhaps with the biblical narrative of the entry into Noah's ark in mind. The painting conveys the mood of tranquillity and harmony. The fallen nature that Tennyson would later characterize as 'red in tooth and claw' is strikingly absent from this highly idealized representation of a long-lost paradise.

And why was it lost? The left-hand side of the picture offers the traditional answer to this question, depicting Eve as plucking fruit from the tree of the knowledge of good and evil. The fruit is represented as apples. Now apples are not mentioned in the Genesis narrative. It is possible that this traditional idea may well have been suggested by the fact that the Latin words for 'apple' and 'evil' are identical (*malum*). For Bruegel, the harmony of nature is about to be wrecked, giving way to the disordered and decayed world that we now know around us. The painting alludes to the tragedy of the human predicament. Somehow, we seem to ruin every paradise, turning our Edens into wastelands.

The Christian hope for the future is shaped in terms of the renewal and transformation of creation. The day will come when 'creation itself will be set free from its bondage to decay' (Romans 8.19–23), and achieve the glorious freedom for which it was created. This theme is reiterated throughout the Old Testament, which frequently looks forward to the final restoration and reintegration of nature. What has been distorted and ruined will be restored to its original integrity – including the animal kingdom:

> The wolf and the lamb shall feed together, the lion shall eat straw like the ox; but the serpent – its food shall be dust! They shall not hurt or destroy on all my holy mountain, says the LORD. (Isaiah 65.25)

In one of his most passionate sermons, the great Methodist preacher and writer John Wesley (1703–91) drew out the implications of such passages for the Christian understanding of heaven. Heaven is not simply about paradise restored, but about paradise transcended through a renewal and perfection of the original creation. As Wesley expressed this hope:

> The whole brute creation will then, undoubtedly, be restored, not only to the vigour, strength, and swiftness which they had at their creation . . . No rage will be found in any creature, no fierceness, no cruelty, or thirst for blood. So far from it that 'the wolf shall dwell with the lamb, the leopard shall lie down with the kid, the calf and the young lion together; and a little child shall lead them. The cow and the bear shall feed together, and the lion shall eat straw like an ox.' (Isaiah 11.6–7)

Lord, help us to care for your work of creation that you have entrusted to us. May we tend the creation as Adam tended Eden, and look forward to the renewal of all things through the coming of your kingdom.

The ideas explored in this chapter demonstrate that we must learn to see nature in a new way, and value it as God's own possession. This must affect the way in which we *behave* towards the created order. Yet it also affects the way in which we *appreciate* creation. In the following chapter, we shall explore the importance of the doctrine of creation for our spirituality.

a spirituality of creation

a spirituality of creation

'Do not be conformed to this world, but be transformed by the renewing of your minds' (Romans 12.2). Paul here sets out two quite different ways of thinking. We can view the world in purely natural terms. Or we can allow the way in which we conceive and understand the world to be transformed by the Christian faith. This gives us a very different reading of things. We now see the world as God's creation, reflecting the divine wisdom and glory, a constant reminder of God's goodness and power. Growing in our faith involves a discipleship of the mind, in which we learn to see things in a new light.

In the previous chapter, we saw how George Herbert's poem 'The elixir' explores the ways in which the Christian faith transforms our perceptions of the world. The Christian doctrine of creation enables us to see the world as God's creation, which is to be loved and tended. Yet Herbert makes other points in that poem, one of which has particular relevance for our thinking about spirituality.

> A man that looks on glass,
> On it may stay his eye;
> Or if he pleaseth, through it pass,
> And then the heaven espy.

We should look through God's creation, in order to behold God himself. To help appreciate his line of thought here, we may explore this image in greater detail.

Herbert proposes that we consider a window as an analogy for Christian doctrine. It is an image that is as familiar to us today as it was in Herbert's time. A window can be considered as a work of art in itself, especially if it is decorated with coloured panes of glass or painted illustrations. We can easily focus our attention on it, appreciating the intricacy of its construction or noticing dust and grime that need to be cleaned away. Yet the window has served its purpose properly only when we look *through* it and see what lies beyond – perhaps one of the exquisite gardens that ornamented the great houses of the early seventeenth century, or a beautiful landscape leading to the mountains in the far distance. If we merely look *at* the window, we miss what lies beyond.

Herbert's analogy has an important implication for thinking about the doctrine of creation. We can allow our eyes to 'stay' on the doctrine itself, and fail to appreciate the new way of seeing things that doctrine makes possible. Theological libraries are full of works dealing with the historical development of the doctrine of creation or the intricacies of some prominent theologian's doctrine of the church. Admittedly, they are not always the most exciting things to read. Nevertheless, they demonstrate that the study of Christian doctrine is not without its merits.

Yet, as we have seen throughout this work, doctrines are like lenses or prisms that make it possible to see things in a new way. We need to look at the world *through* a doctrinal framework, rather than allow ourselves to become fixated on those doctrines themselves. The question that we will consider in this chapter is what difference it makes to see nature as God's creation – in other words, to look upon the world through the prism of the doctrine of creation. Herbert's poem challenges us to avoid being mere theological mechanics, and instead to open our eyes to the new world of ideas that theology makes possible.

We can see the world around us in purely natural terms, treating it (like Isaac Newton) as a giant machine, whose every movement may be analysed and catalogued. We have already seen how William Blake was critical of Newton for this rather rationalist view of the universe, which

neglected the human imagination. Similar criticisms were made by other poets of people who reduced reality to what might be observed and failed to appreciate how nature, if rightly understood, could be seen as a signpost to the transcendent. As God's creation, it acts as a signpost to something greater – to God himself. We see *through* nature – and what we see is God's creation, and hence something of God himself as its creator. There is no suggestion of idolatry in this kind of appreciation of nature. We are admiring the work of God in nature, not worshipping nature, or any of its many aspects, as if it were God.

This point has been made repeatedly by Christian theologians concerned to ensure we fully appreciate the spiritual dimensions of God's creation. An excellent example of this approach can be found in the writings of Bonaventure (1217–74), who gave the Franciscan order intellectual leadership after the death of St Francis himself. Bonaventure had a keen eye for the importance of the creation as a guide to its creator:

> All the creatures of this tangible world lead the soul of the wise and contemplative person to the eternal God, since they are his shadows, echoes and pictures . . . They are set before us for the sake of our knowing God, and are divinely given signs. For every creature is by its very nature a kind of portrayal and likeness of that eternal Wisdom.

Since the world was indeed created by God, Bonaventure argues that the beauty, goodness and wisdom of its creator are reflected, however dimly, in what we see around us. All of us have known a sense of delight at the beauty of the natural world. Yet this is only a shadow of the beauty of its creator. We see what is good and realize that something still better lies beyond it.

And what lies beyond is not an abstract, impersonal and unknowable force, but a personal God who has created us in order to love and cherish us.

It is helpful to see this heightened awareness of the spiritual significance of creation against the growing interest in depicting nature in various schools of painting of the seventeenth and eighteenth centuries. Artists did not need to paint specifically religious topics – such as the crucifixion or annunciation – to give their works spiritual significance. A landscape was in itself a witness to the beauty and wisdom of God. An excellent example of this approach is found in the 1635 work *Landscape with a Rainbow* by Peter Paul Rubens (1577–1640).

A member of the Flemish Baroque School, Rubens often used bold and sumptuous colours to create a sense of drama in his pictures. His personal religious faith found expression in many of his earlier works, particularly classics such as *The Descent from the Cross* (1611) in Antwerp Cathedral. In his later years, he increasingly turned to portraits and landscapes. *Landscape with a Rainbow* demonstrates Rubens' growing concern for depicting moods and atmospheres, rather than simply providing a detailed representation of nature.

Its central feature is a double rainbow, which illuminates the further reaches of the landscape. The rainbow is a good example of a feature of the natural world which has come to have important associations with our grasp of the transcendent. In the Old Testament, the rainbow is seen as a covenant sign – a natural event, which is declared to be 'a sign of the covenant between [God] and the earth' (Genesis 9.13). The rainbow is a sign of the covenant of creation, just as bread and wine are signs of a covenant of redemption. It is an aspect of creation that points firmly to the creator, proclaiming both his handiwork and his promises.

It is entirely right for Christians to delight in nature, seeing it as a reminder and reflection of its creator. Many Christian writers and movements celebrated the beauty of nature as a witness to God. Celtic Christianity, which arose in Ireland and parts of Scotland in the period 500–1000, took a particularly important lead in this matter. Celtic Christians delighted in the wild, elemental aspects of nature, seeing in the great uncontrollable forces of nature powerful witnesses to the limitless power of God. Its leaders advocated a life of simplicity, in close harmony with the God-given state of nature, emphasizing the benefits of loving and encountering the world of nature as a means of knowing God.

One of its best-known works is that ancient Irish hymn traditionally ascribed to Patrick, and known as the 'Deer's Cry'. The hymn shows a fascination with the natural world as a means of knowing God and appreciating God's glory:

> I bind to myself today
> The power of Heaven,
> The light of the sun,
> The brightness of the moon,
> The splendour of fire,
> The flashing of lightning,
> The swiftness of wind,

The depth of sea,
The stability of earth,
The compactness of rocks.

Yet the Celtic vision of nature goes further than a mere respect for the natural order as a witness to God's power. We find here a strong sense of a reciprocal relationship between God and the creation. By living so close to nature, the Celtic Christians could not help being overwhelmed by the sense of the presence of God in nature. The creation seemed to proclaim and extol its creator at every turn. Animals, birds, plants and running water were all seen as hinting at the divine glory. Many Celtic monasteries were situated in remote regions of Ireland, close to nature. The monks had ample time to study nature, and came to love its rich tapestry. As a ninth-century Celtic poem puts it:

Almighty Creator, who has made all things,
The world cannot express all your glories,
Even if the grass and the trees were to sing.

The illustrations in Celtic manuscripts show a concern for the fine details of the natural world. This fascination with the natural order of things was grounded in a belief that it hinted at the greater glory of God, and was a way of drawing closer to that glory. As a work attributed to Ninian of Whithorn argued, the supreme aim of the study of nature is 'to perceive the eternal word of God reflected in every plant and insect, every bird and animal, and every man and woman'. Others echoed this theme, even if their names have been lost to history – such as the author of this short hymn of praise:

> There is no life in the sea,
> No creature in the river,
> Nothing in the heavens,
> That does not proclaim God's goodness.
>
> There is no bird on the wing,
> No star in the sky,
> Nothing beneath the sun,
> That does not proclaim God's goodness.

The doctrine of creation encourages us to throw our whole selves into a spirit of wonder and gratitude as we contemplate the world of nature around us, and see it as having its origins in God, pointing to his wisdom and beauty. We could do far worse than join with our Celtic predecessors in cultivating an attitude of constant appreciation for the artistic majesty that surrounds us each and every day of our lives. We have become so familiar with the creation that we have lost our sense of wonder at its beauty, and our sense of awe at its wonders. Yet these are things that we can – and should! – rediscover.

One of those who tried to do this was Gerard Manley Hopkins (1844–89), hopelessly neglected during his lifetime, yet now recognized as one of the greatest nineteenth-century poets. His poem 'God's grandeur' (1877) is widely regarded as one of the best attempts to convey the sense of wonder evoked by God's creation, and the inability of humanity to destroy this through industrialization and urbanization.

> The world is charged with the grandeur of God.
> It will flame out, like shining from shook foil;
> It gathers to a greatness, like the ooze of oil
> Crushed.

We see here a powerful appeal to the 'baptized imagination' – to see the glory of the Lord shining, flashing and scintillating from his work of creation, even in the midst of the darkness of the human world.

Lord, teach us to see you in all things. Help us to see your wisdom and glory in the silent brilliance of the night sky, the majesty of still blue mountains and the vastness of the oceans. May they move us to praise you and long to know you more.

Yet this raises another question. If the heavens can declare the glory of the Lord, what of other aspects of nature? What about seeds, flowers or birds? To explore this further, we shall begin to think about the 'parables of creation' told by Jesus during his ministry to proclaim the coming of the kingdom of God.

the parables of creation

the parables of creation

A parable, we are often told, is an earthly story with a heavenly meaning. There is, of course, much more that needs to be said about parables than this. Nevertheless, the simplicity of this traditional definition makes it an ideal starting point for our reflections on the importance of the created order for theological and spiritual reflection.

Many of the parables told by Jesus are based on the regular rhythms and everyday events of rural life in Palestine. The way in which seeds grow, the signs of changing weather, the behaviour of birds and animals – all become starting points for Jesus's teaching about the kingdom of God, *if interpreted correctly*. They need to be seen in a certain way. The Hebrew root of the word 'parable' can have the sense of something hidden or mysterious – in other words, something that needs to be explained. Just as the wonders of nature need to be *interpreted* as God's creation, witnessing in some way to God's wisdom and glory, so the parables need to be understood in a certain way before they can proclaim the coming of God's kingdom.

The parables of creation are grounded in an intimate knowledge of the natural world. The crowds that eagerly gathered to hear Jesus's teaching of the kingdom heard analogies and illustrations that related naturally to their everyday lives. He spoke their language and he knew their conceptual worlds. He talked about the yearly cycle of the sowing and harvesting of crops, the problems of ensuring trees bore fruit and the need to be aware of changing weather patterns. The parables of nature speak with immediacy to their audiences, effortlessly connecting up with their experiences.

We must never think of Jesus 'talking down' to ordinary people. One of the great insights of the Christian doctrine of the incarnation is that Jesus entered into the world of humanity and shared its life, thought and experiences. There is no question of his *pretending* to do this. He was able to use that world as a means of communicating the mysteries of the kingdom of God to those who had eyes to see, and ears to hear.

Many western readers of the gospel parables find themselves at a disadvantage here. Modern urban existence means that many Christians have lost the intimate contact with the world of nature that so many of the parables take for granted. A point which would have been intuitively appreciated by their original audiences may now need to be explained before it can be understood properly. Yet all is far from lost. One of the most remarkable things about the 'parables of creation' is that they not only use the world of nature to illuminate the gospel; they allow the gospel to bring about a new interest in the world of creation.

To recognize the power of these parables, we must try to enter into a world which is very different from that many of us know. We must leave behind the world of vast cities, congested roads, car parks and concrete walkways, and enter another world – either physically, by travelling there, or imaginatively, by allowing someone else to lead us there in our minds. There is much to be said for the former. From the beginning of the Christian era, many have aimed to leave behind the pollution, busyness and noise of the city to be closer to God, and renew their appreciation of the gospel in the stillness and solitude of the wilderness. Who can read Thomas Merton (1915–68) without acknowledging how much the natural beauty of the Monastery of Gethsemani, set in rural Kentucky, shaped his thought and his understanding of the gospels?

We shall be adopting the second approach – allowing our imaginations to create the close encounter with the world of creation that the gospel parables envisage, and asking what insights this process of encounter might bring us. To aid us in this venture, we will draw on the experience of someone who left a bustling city to settle for a while in the countryside – Vincent van Gogh (1853–90).

Not many know that as a young man van Gogh developed a passionate interest in Christian theology. In 1869 he became apprenticed to a

firm of Parisian art dealers. This helped him gain both an appreciation of art and a knowledge of the inner workings of the art business. He was transferred to the company's London offices in 1873, and became increasingly fond of England and the English way of life. Eventually, he resigned this position and went to teach at a boys' school in Ramsgate. By the summer of 1876, he realized that he was deeply attracted to the Christian faith. He began to think in terms of ordination. At this time he was teaching at a school in Isleworth run by Thomas Slade Jones, a Congregationalist minister, and exercising a modest pastoral ministry.

On Sunday 29 October 1876, van Gogh preached his first sermon. By all reports, it was not an entirely successful event. His delivery lacked the passion that he clearly felt for his subject but was unable to put into words. Yet in the end it would not be words, but images, that proved to be van Gogh's chosen means of communication. This early sermon vividly displays van Gogh's fundamental belief that art illuminates and inspires faith. Towards the end of the sermon he spoke of the Christian life as a pilgrimage. Rather than develop the intellectual aspects of the concept of such a pilgrimage, he turned to art to make his point.

I once saw a very beautiful picture: it was a landscape at evening. In the distance on the right-hand side a row of hills appeared blue in the evening mist. Above those hills the splendour of the sunset, the grey clouds with their linings of silver and gold and purple. The landscape is a plain or heath covered with grass and its yellow leaves, for it was in autumn. Through the landscape a road leads to a high mountain far, far away, on the top of that mountain is a city wherein the setting sun casts a glory. On the road walks a pilgrim, staff in hand.

Our preacher went on to make some entirely appropriate points about the nature of the Christian life. Yet what has always impressed me as significant here is the way in which van Gogh appeals to the imagination, creating a word-picture which allowed his audience to bring new depth to the traditional image of the believer as a pilgrim, trying to progress through the wilderness of this world.

Nothing much came of van Gogh's hopes for ordination. He pursued theological studies in Amsterdam in 1877, unsuccessfully, before moving to the bleak Borinage region of Belgium to begin a ministry to its coalminers. By the end of 1879 he had become convinced that he was a failure in his chosen area of service and decided to become a professional artist instead. By 1886 he was in Paris, where he formed a turbulent and ultimately fateful friendship with Paul Gauguin, while experimenting with different styles of painting.

Yet our interest focuses on the critical year of 1888, when van Gogh made the momentous decision to leave behind the urban sprawl of Paris and settle in the south of France. He left Paris by train on 20 February, arriving in the town of Arles towards the end of an unusually cold winter. Within weeks, however, winter had given way to spring and the great annual transformation of creation had begun. Some of van Gogh's greatest works date from this period, including his painting *Path through a Field with Willows*. The beauty of the Provence countryside proved an inspiration, as did the activities associated with it – such as sowing seeds.

At least four of van Gogh's paintings from this period bear the title 'the Sower', reflecting the importance of this event for the rural life of the region. Some depict the sower at work in the countryside, labouring under the brilliance of the Provence sun; others depict him against the backdrop of the outskirts of Arles, the smokestacks of its factories contrasting with the simplicities of the rural landscape – and perhaps promoting the unspoken question: when will these fields be swallowed up by industrial expansion?

Yet the most beautiful of van Gogh's sowers was painted in November 1888. It is generally known as *Sower with Setting Sun*. The sower's features are in shadow as he strides away from the setting sun. The late autumn landscape is already showing signs of the approaching winter. Yet the very act of sowing seed is itself a promise of the spring that is to come. I find it difficult to study this picture without being reminded of *The Practice of The Presence of God* by Brother Lawrence of the Resurrection (1611–91). Lawrence tells of an insight he gained at the age of sixteen, which remained with him throughout his life. He found himself contemplating a tree in the depths of winter, stripped bare of its leaves. Yet he knew that, with the coming of spring, 'the leaves would be renewed, and after that the flowers and fruit appear'. It was not something he need worry about. He could trust that renewal would come in its own good time. In the same way, he argues that we should have a settled trust in God, which sustains us in times of spiritual dryness. As Lawrence puts it, we should use both our minds and imaginations to 'establish ourselves in the presence of God'. Is this promise also hinted at by van Gogh? He certainly knew enough about the Gospels to appreciate the importance of the point.

Perhaps we can allow van Gogh's image to stimulate our imaginations as we reflect on one of the great parables of creation found in the fourth chapter of Mark's Gospel. The parable of the sower (Mark 4.1–20) is so familiar to us that we have come to take it for granted. Yet it is a powerful reminder of the way in which events in the natural world help us understand spiritual truths.

> A sower went out to sow. And as he sowed, some seed fell on the path, and the birds came and ate it up. Other seed fell on rocky ground, where it did not have much soil, and it sprang up quickly, since it had no depth of soil. And when the sun rose, it became scorched, and since it had no root, it withered away. Other seed fell among thorns, and the thorns grew up and choked it, and it yielded no grain. Other seed fell into good soil, and brought forth grain, growing up and increasing and yielding thirty and sixty and a hundredfold. And he said, 'Let anyone with ears to hear listen!'

It is easy to imagine the scene, especially with van Gogh's 1888 work as our guide. Picture the sower, walking up and down the fields, sowing the seed.

See in your mind the seed falling on the ground – on the hard, dry path alongside the field; on shallow soil; into the midst of a patch of thorns; and finally on to good, deep soil. The main point that the parable makes so superbly is that it is the same seed that is sown in every case. The outcome depends upon the ground into which it falls.

The implication seems clear: people respond in different ways to the preaching of the gospel message. It has no discernible effect on some. Others respond gladly – but then seem to lose interest. Only in some cases does it truly take root. The parable tells us that there is nothing wrong with the gospel message. Its impact on people depends on whether they provide the right soil in which it may grow. And when the gospel truly takes root, it grows and bears fruit.

The parable of the sower thus provides us with a framework for making sense of how the preaching of the same gospel impacts on people in such different ways. It also offers us a way of critiquing ourselves by inviting us to ask hard questions. For example, what sort of soil are we providing for the gospel seed? Is it like a patch of ground in which other well-established plants are already growing, so that the new seed will be choked? Part of the ongoing agenda of Christian discipleship is to review our priorities and commitments, to see if we have allowed something else to displace God from his proper place.

Martin Luther once offered a helpful way of checking whether we have allowed this to happen. 'Whatever your heart depends upon, and wherever your heart is fixed – that is actually your god.' In other words, asking ourselves what we *really* trust and where our security and affection *really* lie is a highly effective tool for self-critique. And if there are thorns growing in the soil of our lives – to revert to the imagery of the parable – we will need to uproot them to make way for the new wine of the gospel.

4 the parables of creation

Lord, help our seed of faith to grow. May we provide good soil in which it may grow, slowly yet surely. And may we bear fruit, that others may know of the joy and peace of your kingdom.

One of these secrets of the kingdom is that Jesus of Nazareth is none other than the Lord of creation, a theme which we shall explore in the following chapter.

the lord of creation

In the previous chapter, we looked at some examples of the 'parables of creation'. During his ministry, Jesus used many aspects of nature to illuminate some of the great themes of the coming kingdom of God. This might be taken to suggest that Jesus's relationship to nature was passive, as if he were no more than an observer of its patterns, or a shrewd teacher opportunistically exploiting convenient natural features to make a theological point. Yet there is rather more to things than the previous chapter suggested. To make this clear, we shall consider another aspect of Jesus's relationship to the natural order – the miracles of creation.

The Gospel narratives place us alongside the first disciples, as they gradually gain a deepening understanding of who Jesus is. They had left everything in order to heed his call: 'Follow me'. No explanation was given. The force of the command and the personal authority of the one who spoke was enough to compel them to leave all and follow him. But who was he? As the Gospel narratives proceed, we begin to understand. First, we discover the teacher – the one who 'spoke with authority' (Mark 1.27). Yet that authority is soon found to extend to creation itself.

The 'miracles of creation' are an integral part of the gospel accounts of the significance of Jesus Christ. They cast vitally important light on the significance of Jesus by reporting both what happened and the impact that this had on people. For example, consider the healing of the paralytic, one of the earliest miracles recorded in the Gospel accounts (Mark 2.1–12). There is no doubt that something immensely significant took place through the healing itself. Yet the impression created by that miracle must also be appreciated. It was like a signpost, pointing to certain things about Jesus Christ that must be true if he was able to act in this way. The crowd who witnessed the event were 'all amazed and glorified God, saying, "We have never seen anything like this!"' (Mark 2.12)

A further example of this authority is provided by the stilling of the storm on Lake Galilee. Here is Mark's account of this event:

> On that day, when evening had come, [Jesus] said to them, 'Let us go across to the other side.' And leaving the crowd behind them, they took him with them in the boat, just as he was. Other boats were with him. A great gale arose, and the waves beat into the boat, so that the boat was already being swamped. But he was in the stern, asleep on the cushion; and they woke him up and said to him, 'Teacher, do you not care that we are perishing?' He woke up and rebuked the wind, and said to the sea, 'Peace! Be still!' Then the wind ceased, and there was a dead calm. He said to them, 'Why are you afraid? Have you still no faith?' And they were filled with great awe, and said to one another, 'Who then is this, that even the wind and the sea obey him?' (Mark 4.35–41)

This incident has proved a spiritual inspiration to many – for example, the young Vincent van Gogh, who made it a central theme of his first sermon, preached in Isleworth on Sunday 29 October 1876. All who have been buffeted by life's storms could find solace and peace in Christ.

> You who have experienced the great storms of life, you over whom all the waves and all the billows of the Lord have gone – have you not heard, when your heart failed for fear, the beloved well-known voice with something in its tone that reminded you of the voice that charmed your childhood – the voice of Him whose name is Saviour and Prince of Peace, saying as it were to you personally, mind to you personally: 'It is I, be not afraid.'

Fear not. Let not your heart be troubled. And we whose lives have been calm up till now, calm in comparison of what others have felt – let us not fear the storms of life, amidst the high waves of the sea and under the grey clouds of the sky we shall see Him approaching, for whom we have so often longed and watched, Him we need so – and we shall hear His voice: 'It is I, be not afraid.'

Yet there is a deeper point being made here. Any account of the identity of Jesus Christ must give full weight to the gospel accounts of how people responded to what Jesus did. Who, they wondered, must Jesus be if the elements of creation obeyed him? In the Old Testament, the winds and seas were often seen as symbols of deeper forces of chaos, which God was able to control through his mighty power. Yet this ability to *command* nature was also seen in Jesus himself. Who must he be, if he could act in this way? They already knew Jesus as one who taught with authority; they had now to come to terms with his being the Lord of all creation. In some way, creation seemed to be his to command.

The Gospel of John provides the most extended illustration of the authority of Jesus over nature. These acts of authority are *signs* which reveal his previously hidden glory to the world. The changing of the water into wine at Cana in Galilee is described as 'the first of his signs' by which Jesus 'revealed his glory' (John 2.11). Later we encounter the 'second sign that Jesus did' (John 4.54) – the healing of the official's son at Capernaum. We find references to other signs later in the Gospel (John 12.37). Indeed, John provides the following reason for assembling his Gospel:

Now Jesus did many other signs in the presence of his disciples which are not written in this book. But these are written in order that you may come to believe that Jesus is the Messiah, the Son of God, and that through believing you may have life in his name. (John 20.30–31)

This has led some scholars to suggest that one of the sources used by John for his Gospel was a 'book of signs' – in other words, a very early collection of accounts of Jesus's healings and miracles, in circulation at a very early stage. These signs confirm and proclaim Jesus's authority over the world of creation. Most scholars believe that there are seven such 'signs', as follows:

1   The changing of water into wine (John 2.1–11)
2   The healing of the official's son (John 4.46–54)
3   The healing of the lame man (John 5.2–9)
4   The feeding of the multitude (John 6.1–14)
5   The restoration of sight to a blind man (John 9.1–7)
6   The raising of Lazarus (John 11.1–45)
7   The resurrection of Jesus himself (John 20.1–29)

All seven involve Jesus demonstrating his authority over the natural world.

In view of its importance for our theme, we shall examine the first of these signs in more detail. The story of the wedding at Cana in Galilee was highly attractive to artists, and became the subject of many pictures of the Middle Ages and Renaissance. It is the subject, for example, of a particularly fine fresco by Giotto in the Scrovegni Chapel in Padua, painted over the period 1303–5. One representation of this event, however, stands out for its beauty and symbolism. It is by the Flemish painter Juan de Flandes (born 1465), who was active in Spain over the period 1496–1519. This was a highly significant period of revival and renewal within the Spanish Church, supported by Ferdinand and Isabella of Spain. It was also a time of renaissance within Spanish arts as a whole, supported to no small extent by Isabella herself. Juan de Flandes was one of a group of northern artists whom Isabella appointed to positions within her court. Among his many works were depictions of some core events described in John's Gospel, including the encounter between Christ and the woman of Samaria, and the raising of Lazarus.

In 1500, Juan de Flandes executed his study of the wedding at Cana in oil on wood. The painting is a superb aid to interaction with this biblical passage. The main figures in the painting are Jesus and his mother Mary on the left, and the groom and bride towards its centre. According to John, Jesus and his new disciples were invited to the wedding. Having heard Jesus speak, they knew that there was something special about him (John 1.35–51). But *what*? As things worked out, events at the wedding advanced their understanding of this question considerably.

The story centres on how a major social embarrassment was averted. The wedding party had run out of wine. Contemporary Jewish sources often stress the importance of providing adequate supplies of wine, occasionally hinting that even rabbis were known to drink deeply on such occasions. The host would have failed his guests if he did not supply enough wine. He would be seen as stingy, ill-prepared and unappreciative of those invited to share the joy of the day.

John draws our attention to the presence of 'the mother of Jesus' at the wedding, who tactfully draws his attention to the problem that has arisen. Jesus's reply – 'My hour has not yet come' – has provoked much discussion. Perhaps it is best understood as meaning that the time of his final glorification through the resurrection has yet to come. What we see in the miracle of creation that is about to take place should thus be understood as an *anticipation* of the disclosure of his resurrected glory. It is a hint of the greater glory that is to be revealed, and a preparation of the minds and hearts of his disciples to receive it.

Jesus asks that the water required for ritual purification be brought to him in containers. Juan de Flandes represents him as making a gesture at this point, raising his hand in an act of blessing or of authority. Our eye is drawn initially to the towels already placed on the table in preparation for this washing, and then to the servant who is pouring out wine from one of five (the Gospel account mentions six) large stone water-jars. Something remarkable has happened. Yet the newly married couple beside him, to judge by the expression on their faces, know nothing either of the problem or its remarkable solution. Nor does the steward, who compliments them on holding back the best wine until the end.

So what does this sign mean? To what does it point? First, we must note that this was a private sign, given to the disciples and those in Jesus's immediate circle; the public signs will come later. The disciples, who up to this point knew Jesus as a commanding presence and charismatic figure, now discover something of the secret of his Lordship. The episode is an important milestone along the road of discipleship, as Jesus's first followers come to behold his glory.

Yet the significance of the event reaches far beyond its impact on those first disciples. It helps us explore the relation of the worlds of creation and redemption. The 'sign' takes place within the world of nature, yet points beyond that world of nature. The hope of redemption and glory is disclosed through the created order.

There is a linear trajectory of divine action and involvement – which theologians often like to refer to as the 'economy of salvation' – from creation through redemption to the final consummation of all things. (The word 'economy' derives from a Greek word meaning 'the way a household is organized'.) God, having created the world, moves on to recreate it after it had lost its way, and fallen into ruin and decay. This idea of the 'economy of salvation' helps us to make sense of the relation of creation and redemption; the turning of water into wine enables the imagination to make that same connection, yet at a deeper level.

For redemption is not simply about the *restoration* of nature to its original state; it is about its *transformation*. The water of the created order is transformed into the wine of the order of redemption. There is nothing wrong with water; it is just that wine is better. Traditional Christian theology has always declared that the redeemed life exceeds in wonder the life of innocence. In other words, redemption places us beyond where creation left us. God, in redeeming us, does not return us to the 'GO' of the Monopoly Board of life; he moves us onwards and upwards. In Judaism, an abundance of wine was seen as a defining characteristic of the long-awaited messianic age (Amos 9.13; Hosea 14.7; Joel 4.18). John's account of the incident at Cana implies that this age has dawned. Something good gives way to something better.

And, in case anyone should miss the obvious connections between redemption and the death of Christ, Juan de Flandes places a loaf of bread on the table, directly above the jars of new wine. The bread and wine remind us immediately of the suffering and death of Christ and his command to remember him through these physical elements. The picture can therefore also be seen as a reminder of Christ's promise to be present with his people at table through the bread and wine.

Lord, help us to be like those first disciples, whose knowledge and understanding deepened as they came to know you better. May we too know you through the breaking of bread, and experience the water of our lives transformed into the wine of your kingdom.

We have already begun to touch on the whole area of the redemption of humanity and its restoration to glory through Christ. Yet to make sense of this we must now turn to explore a further area of the Christian doctrine of creation – namely, the Christian view that humanity has been made in the 'image of God'.

the place of humanity in creation

'What are human beings, that you are mindful of them?' (Psalm 8.4) From the beginning of history, people have wondered about their place in the greater scheme of things. Why are we here? What is our destiny? What is the meaning of human existence? The doctrine of creation offers the beginnings of an answer. It helps us to deepen our understanding and appreciation of the world in which we find ourselves placed.

We are part of God's creation, and must learn and accept our place within that created order. This insight is deeply countercultural and often provokes a ferocious reaction. Some argue that the world would be a better place if we got rid of God altogether and put human beings in his place. Many of the more idealistic writers of the nineteenth century insisted that the only way to eliminate the ills of the world was to enthrone humanity as lord of the earth. After the horrors of the earlier twentieth century, which saw Nazism and Stalinism built on precisely this exalted view of humanity, a more realistic approach has returned to favour.

Yet although Christians believe that humanity is part of the created order, this does not mean that we are *indistinguishable* from the remainder of creation. We have been set a little lower than the angels and been 'crowned with glory and honour' (Psalm 8.5). Men and women are created 'in the image of God' (Genesis 1.27). This brief yet deeply significant phrase opens the way to a right understanding of human nature and our overall place within the created order. Although humanity is not divine, it possesses a relationship with God which is different from that of other creatures. *Humanity bears the image of God.* For some, this is a statement of the privileged position of humanity within creation. Yet for most Christian theologians, it is above all an affirmation of *responsibility* and *accountability* towards the world in which we live.

So how are we to understand this relationship to God? How can we visualize it? A number of models have been developed within Christian theology, of which we may note three. Each is worth close scrutiny in its own right.

First, the 'image of God' can be seen as a reminder of the authority of God over humanity. In the ancient Near East, monarchs would often display images of themselves as an assertion of their power in a region (see, for example, the golden statue of Nebuchadnezzar, described in Daniel 3.1–7). This is familiar to lovers of English poetry through Percy Bysshe Shelley's poem 'Ozymandias'. The poet tells how he heard a traveller's tale from an ancient land of a great statue which lay fallen in the middle of the vastness of the desert sands. Only its pedestal remained, with these once proud words engraved:

> 'My name is Ozymandias, King of Kings,
> Look on my Works ye Mighty, and despair!'
> Nothing beside remains. Round the decay
> Of that colossal Wreck, boundless and bare
> The lone and level sands stretch far away.

The poem is a powerful witness to the fragility of power. As the Old Testament prophets never ceased to point out, God's authority endured, where that of secular rulers passed into the dust.

To be created in the 'image of God' could therefore be understood as being *accountable to God*. This important point underlies an incident in the ministry of Jesus Christ (Luke 20.22–25). Challenged as to whether it was right for Jews to pay taxes to the Roman authorities, Jesus requested that a coin be brought to him. He asked, 'Whose image and title does it bear?' Those standing around replied that it was Caesar's. Christ then tells the

crowd to give to Caesar what is Caesar's, and to God what is God's. While some might take this to be an evasion of the question, it is nothing of the sort. It is a reminder that those who bear God's image – that is, humanity – must dedicate themselves to him.

Second, the idea of the 'image of God' can be taken to refer to some kind of correspondence between human reason and the rationality of God as creator. On this understanding of things, there is an intrinsic resonance between the structures of the world and human reasoning. This approach is set out with particular clarity in Augustine's major theological writing *On the Trinity*:

> The image of the creator is to be found in the rational or intellectual soul of humanity . . . [The human soul] has been created according to the image of God in order that it may use reason and intellect in order to apprehend and behold God.

For Augustine, we have been created with the intellectual resources which can set us on the way to finding God by reflecting on the creation.

In more recent years, the importance of this point has been explored by the physicist turned theologian John Polkinghorne, formerly professor of mathematical physics at Cambridge University. Polkinghorne points out that some of the most beautiful patterns thought up by the mathematicians are found actually to occur in the structure of the physical world around us. There seems to be some deep-seated relationship between the reason within (the rationality of our minds – in this case mathematics) and the reason without (the rational order and structure of the physical world around us). The two fit together like a glove. So why are our minds so perfectly shaped to understand the deep patterns of the world around us?

the place of humanity in creation

For Polkinghorne, we need to understand why the 'reason within' and the 'reason without' fit together at a deep level. Christian belief provides us, he argues, with a rational and entirely satisfying explanation of that fact. It affirms that the 'reason within' and the 'reason without' have a common origin in this deeper rationality which is the reason of God the Creator, whose will is the ground of both our mental and our physical experience of the world.

Polkinghorne argues that there seems to be some kind of 'resonance' or 'harmonization' between the ordering of the world and the capacity of the human mind to discern and represent it:

> If the deep-seated congruence of the rationality present in our minds with the rationality present in the world is to find a true explanation, it must surely lie in some more profound reason which is the ground of both. Such a reason would be provided by the Rationality of the Creator.

A third approach suggests that the 'image of God' is about the capacity to relate to God. To be created in the 'image of God' is to possess the potential to enter into a relationship with God. The term 'image' here expresses the idea that God has created humanity with a specific goal – namely, to relate to God. This theme has played a major role in Christian spirituality, as will become clear presently, when we explore this idea in greater detail. But first, let us lay the background to this discussion by reflecting on one of the best-known images in the history of art – Michelangelo's painting of the creation of Adam.

The Sistine Chapel is one of the most remarkable buildings in Europe. It was constructed during the pontificate of Sixtus VI over the period

1475–83, according to a design by Baccio Pontelli. The dimensions of the building were modelled on the Temple of Solomon, as described in detail in the Old Testament (1 Kings 5—8, 2 Kings 25.13–17, 2 Chronicles 2—4). The building is rectangular in shape and measures 40.93 metres long by 13.41 metres wide, corresponding to what was then the best interpretation of the biblical measurements, which were given in cubits.

Once the building was constructed, careful thought was given to its decoration. The walls were richly illustrated with scenes from the Gospels by such leading painters as Pietro Perugino (*c.* 1450–1524) and Bernardino Pinturicchio (1454–1513). Yet for many, it is the painted ceiling which represents the most visually exciting aspect of the building. These paintings, containing some 300 figures, were executed by Michelangelo (1475–1564) over the years 1508–12. Although his original commission was merely to depict the twelve apostles, his vivid imagination and artistic skills led him to create something altogether more awesome and majestic. Michelangelo was primarily known for his superb sculptures (such as his statue of David, 1501–4), but his work in the Sistine Chapel demonstrates his great talent as a painter. Recent renovation work has brought out the remarkable brilliance of his colours, and led to a new appreciation of the vision that lay behind his designs.

A significant part of the work is given over to the narrative of creation, based on the first two chapters of the book of Genesis. Perhaps the most famous of all these illustrations dates from 1511–12, and depicts the creation of humanity. It has become one of the best-known images in the world. Michelangelo did not give the painting a specific title, and it is open to question whether the traditional designation is appropriate. Adam has, in one sense, already been created. Something rather more profound is now taking place.

As art historians have pointed out, Michelangelo depicts Adam as lying languidly and passively. He already exists; what is missing is any *vitality* on his part. The initiative in whatever is happening clearly lies with God, not Adam. God actively reaches out his hand towards Adam, and gives him something which *energizes* him. What is it? The Genesis account itself speaks of God forming Adam, and then breathing life into him (Genesis 2.7). The act of physical formation is thus distinguished from that of spiritual activation. Michelangelo does not depict God breathing into Adam's nostrils, perhaps concerned that such an illustration might be interpreted inappropriately. Yet the resulting picture conveys in a highly vivid manner the total dependence of humanity upon God for its existence.

Yet there is more to Michelangelo's theological artistry than this. Notice how Adam is reaching out towards God. This gesture is itself an important statement about the ultimate goal of human existence. We must consider ourselves to have been created in order to relate to God. Augustine expressed this idea in a famous prayer to God, which has found its way into countless liturgies: 'You have made us for yourself, and our hearts are restless until they find their rest in you.'

Anselm of Canterbury (1033–1109), one of the greatest thinkers of the Middle Ages, prayed along similar lines: 'Lord, give me what you have made me want; I praise and thank you for the desire that you have inspired; perfect what you have begun, and grant me what you have made me long for.'

For these writers, the deep human sense of longing has its origins in God, and can only find its fulfilment in God. God is the name of the one we have been looking for all our lives, without knowing it. God creates a longing for him within our hearts; and then makes himself known and available so that we may encounter him, and finally achieve that joy for which we were created. We are created in such a way that we are bound to extend our hands to find God.

We are thus meant to exist in a relationship with our creator and redeemer. As C. S. Lewis argued, if we do not do this, there is an absence where there ought to be a presence. There is a God-shaped gap within us, which only God can fill. And in his absence, we experience a deep sense of longing – a longing which is really for God, but which fallen and sinful humanity misreads, accidentally or deliberately, as a longing for things within the world. And these things never satisfy. If we are made for God, and God alone, then there is nothing else that will satisfy. And, as Lewis constantly pointed out, this God-given sense of longing provides a key to answering the great questions of life with which humanity has wrestled.

But Michelangelo's deeply evocative image can be read at a third level.

Notice how Adam extends an empty, open hand towards God. He has nothing to offer, but everything to receive. Is this not a helpful way of thinking about our ultimate dependence on God? It is certainly a way of thinking about our relationship to God that many great Christian writers have found helpful. Martin Luther might be mentioned here. Luther died in the early morning of 18 February 1546, having drafted much of a sermon he hoped to preach later. The last words he wrote make this point very powerfully: 'We are beggars. This is true.' We are dependent upon a generous God for everything, and must reach out to him in faith and hope, in order that we may receive from him.

Yet there is a fourth way in which this stunning image from the Sistine Chapel can be viewed. On this approach, God is extending his hand towards Adam to bring Adam to where God is. In other words, the image is a statement of the ultimate destiny of humanity – to be with God in heaven. It is about the hope of future redemption, as much as the celebration of past creation.

Lord, may we take hold of your hand, stretched out towards us, and know your strength and presence in our lives. Help us to live and behave as those who bear your image, and seek to proclaim your glory.

In the next chapter, we shall explore why redemption is such an important issue, as we consider the question of the fall of humanity and its implications.

the ruin and the restoration of humanity

When I was young, I used to enjoy reading stories before going to sleep at night. The great tales from the Brothers Grimm – suitably sanitized, of course – held me in suspense. They and the many other children's stories that I loved at that age made a powerful appeal to my imagination, forcing me to create pictures in my mind as I listened to what was being read to me. Back in the 1950s, few books had illustrations, and I had to create my own imaginary worlds and populate them with imaginary people as I read.

Somehow, the passing of time has softened many of those stories, and my memories of them are probably tinged with a warmth that they lacked. But somehow, so many of them seemed to begin with the words 'Once upon a time . . .' and end with '. . . And they all lived happily ever after.' It was a vastly optimistic view of life, which did little to prepare me for the rather harsher realities I later encountered. Yet it was a world I gladly inhabited and accepted.

One of the great questions of Christian theology is why the creation story doesn't end like that. Why didn't Adam and Eve live happily ever after in the paradise of Eden? Once upon a time they were created; why didn't they just live happily ever after? They had everything they could have wished for – food, water, natural beauty and the presence of God in the cool of the day. Yet this was not good enough. Something was missing. Humanity was present in creation as a creature, not as its Lord. Unwilling to accept the limitations placed upon them by virtue of being human, they chose to rebel against their position within the order of things. Latent within human nature is an unwillingness to accept this order and our place within it. Humanity is an eternal rebel, wanting more and constantly challenging boundaries. Some would argue that this restlessness and desire to overcome any limitations is part of being human.

For many theologians, the essence of the human predicament is our

deep-seated longing to be God. We are unwilling to accept things as they are. We want to have more – and we want to be in charge. Two incidents from the book of Genesis are widely seen as offering a superb commentary on the profound contradictions within human nature – eating the fruit of the 'tree of the knowledge of good and evil', and the construction of the Tower of Babel. Each deserves close attention.

Genesis tells how Adam and Eve were placed within their paradise, and given complete freedom to eat of all its trees – except one (Genesis 2.15–17). This limitation on their freedom proves too much for them. If they were to eat the fruit of the 'tree of the knowledge of good and evil', they would become like God himself, determining what is good and what is evil (Genesis 3.1–5). In part, this incident speaks of the pleasures of eating forbidden fruit. There is something about being prohibited from doing something that makes us long to do it. After all, we reason, it must be *very* special if it is forbidden.

But there is something much deeper here – the human longing to be in charge, to be like God, to make the rules. We long for autonomy; we do not want to be accountable to *anyone*. As the great Russian novelist Fyodor Dostoevsky pointed out in his novel *The Devils* (1871–2), if there is no God, we are able to do as we please. This was one of the great themes of the 'golden age of atheism', which began with the French Revolution in 1789 and ended with the fall of the Berlin Wall in 1989. This period witnessed the great revolt against God, which many historians argue led directly to the horrors of Nazism and Stalinism.

Much the same theme is found in the account of the Tower of Babel (Genesis 11.1–9). This is memorably depicted in the great painting of Pieter Bruegel the Elder (1563), which represents the tower as a giant construction reaching up into the heavens. Its highest regions are lost in the clouds,

reaching out to allow people to touch the face of God. And work is still in progress! Notice the scaffolding on its upper structures. It can reach still higher!

Karl Barth, one of the twentieth century's greatest theologians, saw in this construction another aspect of sinful human nature – the desire to assert human authority and power in the face of God. Barth suggested that the Tower of Babel could be interpreted as a symbol of the human longing to be able to have knowledge of God on our own terms. Instead of waiting for God to reveal himself in terms of his own choosing, humanity believed it could take charge of things and peep into heaven as it pleased. Yet this desire for human control contained within itself the seeds of its own negation. When we take charge, we seem to mess things up.

Over the years, Christian theologians have developed a series of images to help make sense of this puzzling human predicament. Two of the most interesting are *deflection* and *defection*. For the second-century writer Irenaeus of Lyons, humanity has been deflected from its true path by sin. We have lost our way and need to be helped back on to the right road. Irenaeus tends to see humanity as weak and easily misled. We were created as infants, not as mature human beings, and must learn and grow. Asked why God did not create humanity already endowed with perfection, Irenaeus replied that they were simply not ready to cope with it. 'A mother is able to offer food to an infant, but the infant is not yet able to receive food unsuited to its age.'

For Augustine, humanity has defected from its true calling. Instead of using our God-given freedom to love God, we used it to advance our own agendas. We are now caught in a trap of our own making: Augustine argues that we are unable to break free from our entanglement with sin. As Paul points out, we are captivated by indwelling sin, unable to do the good that we would like to do, and instead doing the bad things we do not want to do

the ruin and the restoration of humanity

(Romans 7.17–25). Our only hope lies in being set free by God himself. The freedom to love that ought to have led to fellowship with God – as Adam and Eve walked with God in the garden of Eden – led instead to self-love and a desertion of God for the lesser good.

Augustine uses a series of images to illuminate how we have become trapped by sin in this way. It is like an illness we have contracted and are unable to cure. It is like having fallen into a deep pit and being unable to get out. The essential point he wants to make is that once sin – which he conceives as an active force in our lives – has taken hold of us, we are unable to break free from its grasp. To use a modern analogy, it is like being addicted to heroin and unable to break the habit.

The great English poet John Donne reflects these ideas faithfully in his *Divine Meditations*. Left to our own devices, we cannot be deflected from the path of death and decay. We simply do not have the strength to resist sin and are incapable of breaking free from its stranglehold. Using a rich range of imagery, Donne builds up a picture of humanity being trapped. We are ill and cannot cure ourselves; we are held captive and cannot break free; we are set on a wrong course from which we cannot be deflected. This is best seen in his poem 'Batter my heart, three person'd God', widely regarded as one of his finest, in which Donne stimulates the 'baptized imagination' using a powerful and provocative image.

> Batter my heart, three person'd God; for, you
> As yet but knock, breathe, shine, and seek to mend;
> That I may rise, and stand, o'erthrow me, and bend
> Your force, to break, blow, burn and make me new.
> I, like an usurpt town, to another due,
> Labour to admit you, but Oh, to no end,

Reason your viceroy in me, me should defend,
But is captiv'd, and proves weak or untrue.
Yet dearly I love you, and would be loved fain,
But am betroth'd unto your enemy:
Divorce me, untie, or break that knot again;
Take me to you, imprison me, for I
Except you enthrall me, never shall be free,
Nor ever chaste, except you ravish me.

The basic image is that of the human heart as a town which has fallen captive to an enemy and must be recaptured. The paradox of grace is that God must 'overthrow' and 'bend' us before we can 'rise, and stand'. Our freedom depends upon being 'imprisoned' by God. As one who has been taken prisoner by sin, Donne pleads that he might be taken captive by the one he loves – God himself. He welcomes the thought of the door of his life being battered down, so that God might enter to renew his soul and rebuild the ruins of his broken life.

But already our thoughts are moving on from creation to the *restoration* of that creation through redemption. How can humanity be liberated from its entrapment to sin? How can fallen human nature be restored? How can sin be displaced or forcibly ejected from our lives? The

answer to such questions is as rich as it is wonderful, and is the subject of other volumes in this series. But we may hint at part of the answer by returning to Bruegel's beautiful illustration of the Tower of Babel. This edifice is a symbol of one of the most basic natural human beliefs about God. To find God, we must climb into the heavens. Gaining access to God only comes about through our own efforts. Yet the gospel contradicts this. God chose to come down and dwell among us, bypassing our efforts to find him by ourselves. We prefer to build our Towers of Babel as places of safety and security. It seems more reasonable to trust in ourselves rather than in God as our tower and refuge (Psalm 18.2). Yet God frustrates our misguided efforts to find him, and instead comes in search of us.

In his poem 'Man', George Herbert develops this powerful yet profoundly counter-intuitive idea of incarnation – the idea that God enters into human history and human life, in order to transform them.

> My God, I heard this day
> That none doth build a stately habitation,
> But he that means to dwell therein.

What house more stately hath there been,
Or can be, than is Man? to whose creation
All things are in decay.

Herbert begins by noting that humanity has been created to be inhabited by God. We see here an intensification of the idea developed by Augustine: that we have been made to *relate* to God. Herbert's theme is already found in the New Testament, which speaks of believers as 'temples of the Holy Spirit' (1 Corinthians 6.19–20).

Yet human nature, intended to be the height of God's creation, lies in ruins. It is in need of radical remodelling and internal renewal. Like a once great palace fit for a king, it has fallen into disrepair and decay. Yet Herbert knows that the situation can be redeemed. God's presence itself within human nature would bring about the renewal and restoration of, and make pristine again, what was now languishing in sin and death. If God were to enter into the human situation, it could be transformed from within.

Since then, my God, thou hast
So brave a palace built, O dwell in it
That it may dwell with thee at last!

In these brief lines, Herbert sketches the outline of a doctrine of the incarnation – the idea that God went into our world and our history as one of us, in order to bring us to heaven. He came into our habitation, in order that we might enter his – not as interlopers, but as welcome and honoured guests.

7 the ruin and the restoration of humanity

Lord, we thank you for not abandoning us in sin, but loving us and restoring us to yourself. Help us to break free from our remaining sin, and enfold us in your tender care.

It is this great theme of Jesus Christ as God incarnate that we explore in a companion volume in this series. Its title? *Incarnation.*

for further reading

Introductory

*The following are suitable for those approaching the doctrine of creation for the
first time.*

Fergusson, David A. S., *The Cosmos and the Creator: An Introduction to the
    Theology of Creation.* London: SPCK, 1998.
McGrath, Alister E., *Christian Theology: An Introduction*, 3rd edn. Oxford/Cambridge,
    MA: Blackwell Publishers, 2001.
Polkinghorne, John and Michael Welker, *Faith in the Living God.* London: SPCK;
    Minneapolis: Fortress Press, 2001.

More advanced

Barr, James, *Biblical Faith and Natural Theology.* Oxford: Clarendon Press, 1993.
Begbie, Jeremy S., *Voicing Creation's Praise: Towards a Theology of the Arts.* Edinburgh:
    T. & T. Clark, 1991.
Berry, R. J., ed., *The Care of Creation.* Leicester: Inter-Varsity Press, 2000.
Gunton, Colin E., *Christ and Creation.* Grand Rapids, MI: Eerdmans, 1992.
Hauerwas, Stanley, *With the Grain of the Universe: The Church's Witness and Natural
    Theology.* London: SCM Press, 2002.
Kretzmann, Norman, *The Metaphysics of Creation: Aquinas's Natural Theology in
    Summa Contra Gentiles II.* Oxford: Clarendon Press, 1999.
May, Gerhard, *Creatio Ex Nihilo: The Doctrine of 'Creation out of Nothing' in Early
    Christian Thought.* Edinburgh: T. & T. Clark, 1995.
McFague, Sallie, *The Body of God: An Ecological Theology.* London: SCM; Minneapolis:
    Fortress Press, 1993.

McGrath, Alister, *Scientific Theology*, 3 vols. London: Continuum; Grand Rapids, MI: Eerdmans, 2001-2003.

Moltmann, Jürgen, *God in Creation: A New Theology of Creation and the Spirit of God*. Minneapolis: Fortress Press, 1990.

Oeschlaeger, Max, *Caring for Creation: An Ecumenical Approach to the Environmental Crisis*. New Haven: Yale University Press, 1994.

Pannenberg, Wolfhart, 'The Doctrine of Creation and Modern Science', *Zygon* 23 (1988): 3–21.

Peacocke, Arthur, *Theology for a Scientific Age: Being and Becoming – Natural, Divine, and Human*. Minneapolis: Fortress Press, 1993.

Peters, Ted, ed., *Bridging Science and Religion*. London: SCM; Minneapolis: Fortress Press, 2003.

Polkinghorne, John, *Science and Christian Belief: Theological Reflections of a Bottom-up Thinker*. London: SPCK, 1994/*The Faith of a Physicist: Reflections of a Bottom-up Thinker*. Minneapolis: Fortress Press, 1996.

Polkinghorne, John, *Science and Creation: The Search for Understanding*. London: SPCK, 1988.

Polkinghorne, John, *Science and Theology*. London: SPCK; Minneapolis: Fortress Press, 1998.

Ward, Keith, *Religion and Creation*. Oxford: Oxford University Press, 1996.

Weaver, John, *Earthshaping, Earthkeeping: A Doctrine of Creation*. London: SPCK, 1999.

Welker, Michael, *Creation and Reality*. Minneapolis: Fortress Press, 1999.

illustrations

The Ancient of Days by William Blake (1757–1827), British Museum, London,
UK/Bridgeman Art Library.

Adam and Eve in Paradise, c. 1610–15 (oil on panel) by Jan Bruegel (1601–78) and
Peter Paul Rubens (1577–1640), Mauritshuis, The Hague, The Netherlands/
Bridgeman Art Library.

Landscape with a Rainbow by Peter Paul Rubens (1577–1640), Hermitage,
St Petersburg, Russia/Bridgeman Art Library.

The Sower, 1888 (oil on canvas) by Vincent van Gogh (1853–90), E. G. Buhrle
Collection, Zurich, Switzerland.

The Marriage Feast at Cana by Juan de Flandes (c. 1465–1519), Christie's Images,
London, UK/Bridgeman Art Library.

Sistine Chapel Ceiling, 1508–12: The *Creation of Adam*, 1511–12 (fresco) (post-
restoration) by Michelangelo Buonarroti (1475–1564), Vatican Museums and
Galleries, Vatican City, Italy/Bridgeman Art Library.

Tower of Babel, 1563 (oil on panel) by Pieter Bruegel the Elder (c. 1515–69),
Kunsthistorisches Museum, Vienna, Austria/Bridgeman Art Library.